Holi

FESTIVALS
AROUND THE WORLD

Grace Jones

AV² provides enriched content that supplements and complements this book. Weigl's AV² books strive to create inspired learning and engage young minds in a total learning experience.

Your AV² Media Enhanced books come alive with...

Audio
Listen to sections of the book read aloud.

Key Words
Study vocabulary, and complete a matching word activity.

Video
Watch informative video clips.

Quizzes
Test your knowledge.

Embedded Weblinks
Gain additional information for research.

Slide Show
View images and captions, and prepare a presentation.

Try This!
Complete activities and hands-on experiments.

... and much, much more!

Go to www.av2books.com, and enter this book's unique code.

BOOK CODE

L B V 9 2 8 9 3

AV² by Weigl brings you media enhanced books that support active learning.

Published by AV² by Weigl
350 5th Avenue, 59th Floor New York, NY 10118
Website: www.av2books.com

Library of Congress Cataloging-in-Publication Data

Names: Jones, Grace, 1990- author.
Title: Holi / Grace Jones.
Description: New York : AV2 by Weigl, 2018. I Series: Festivals around the world
Identifiers: LCCN 2018003637 (print) I LCCN 2018009556 (ebook) I ISBN 9781489678034 (Multi User ebook) I ISBN 9781489678010 (hardcover : alk. paper) I ISBN 9781489678027 (softcover)
Subjects: LCSH: Holi (Hindu festival)--Juvenile literature.
Classification: LCC BL1239.82.H65 (ebook) I LCC BL1239.82.H65 J66 2018 (print) I DDC 294.5/36--dc23
LC record available at https://lccn.loc.gov/2018003637

Printed in the United States of America in Brainerd, Minnesota
1 2 3 4 5 6 7 8 9 0 22 21 20 19 18

032018
120417

Project Coordinator: Heather Kissock   Designer: Ana María Vidal

First published by Book Life in 2017

Weigl acknowledges Getty Images, Alamy, Shutterstock, and iStock as the primary image suppliers for this title.

2

Holi

FESTIVALS AROUND THE **WORLD**

Contents

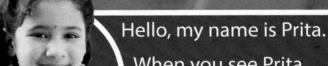

Hello, my name is Prita.

When you see Prita, she will tell you how to say a word.

3

What Is a Festival?

A festival takes place when people come together to celebrate a special event or time of the year. Some festivals last for only one day and others can go on for many months.

Some people celebrate festivals by having a party with their family and friends. Others celebrate by holding special events, performing dances or playing music.

Holi is called the "**Festival of Colors.**"

Prita says:
BRA-MUN (Brahman)

What Is Hinduism?

Hinduism is a religion that began in India over four thousand years ago. Hindus believe in one god called Brahman. However, Hindus often pray to many different gods and goddesses whom they believe are forms of Brahman.

Hindus pray to their different gods and goddesses in a temple called a mandir. Before they enter a mandir, each person must wash so they are clean and remove their shoes as a sign of respect to God.

What Is Holi?

Holi is a festival that is celebrated by Hindus in the spring of every year.

Hindus come together to celebrate the start of spring. They celebrate by lighting large bonfires and covering their friends and family in brightly colored powder and water.

Holi celebrations usually last for **two days**.

The Story of Holi

A long, long time ago in India, there was once a great king called Hiranyakashyap. He wanted his people to worship him like a god.

His son, Prahlad, refused and continued to worship the Hindu god Vishnu. The cruel king punished his son, but still he refused to worship the king.

Prita says:
PRA-LAD (Prahlad)
VISH-NOO (Vishnu)

The king's sister, a witch named Holika, decided to help the king. She tricked Prahlad into sitting on a burning fire. Holika told him that her magic would protect him.

As the flames grew higher, Vishnu took Prahlad from the fire and saved him from harm. His wicked aunt, Holika, died.

Prahlad felt sorry for his aunt and promised to name a festival after her. The Holi festival is named after Prahlad's aunt, Holika.

The lighting of bonfires at Holi is known as **Holika Dahan**.

Prita says:
HO-LEE-KA DA-HAN
(Holika Dahan)

12

Lighting Bonfires

On the first day of Holi, after the sun has set, Hindus light bonfires to remind them of Holika's story. It is also done to celebrate Prahlad's faith in God.

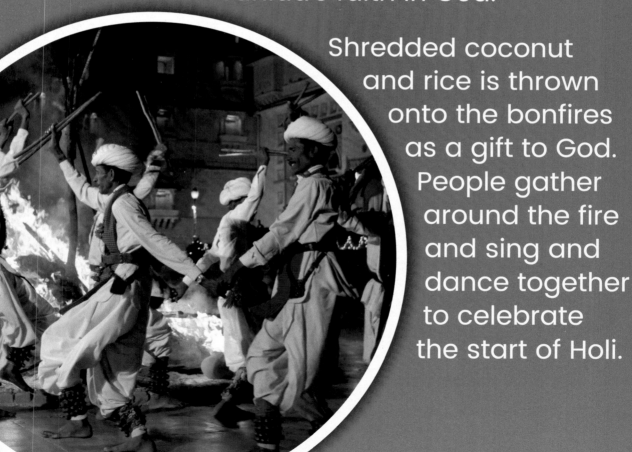

Shredded coconut and rice is thrown onto the bonfires as a gift to God. People gather around the fire and sing and dance together to celebrate the start of Holi.

Festival of Colors

The day after the Holika bonfire, people celebrate Holi by throwing colored powder and water over each other. They use their hands, balloons and even water guns to cover people in color!

Holi is a time of festive fun, laughter and enjoyment. People play jokes on each other to celebrate the playful God Krishna. Legend has it that Krishna once played a trick on a group of milkmaids by covering them in colored water.

Prita says:
People wish each other "Holi Mubarak" (HO-LEE MOO-BAH-RAK) which means "Happy Holi" in Hindi.

15

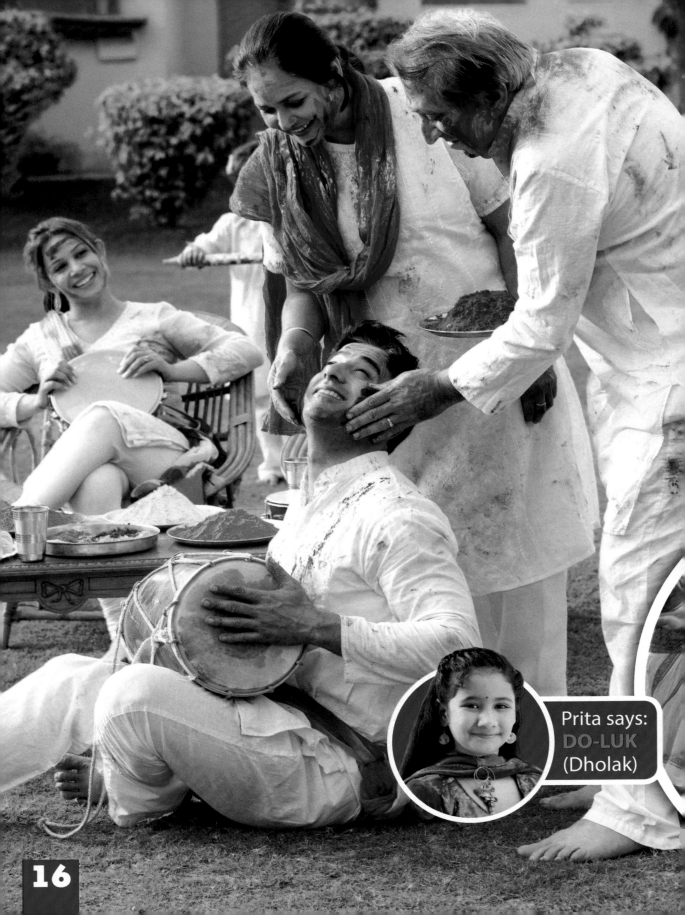

Prita says:
DO-LUK
(Dholak)

Music and Dancing

People fill the streets with joyful singing and lively dancing to celebrate Holi together as a community. People perform dances, plays and songs that act out the stories of Holika and Krishna.

Traditional instruments, like the dholak, are played in the streets. A dholak is a traditional hand drum. People also blow whistles and sing during the festival.

Festive Food

People clean the colors off themselves and come together with their family and friends to eat traditional festival food. In India, gujiya—sweet dumplings filled with dry fruit and coconut—are eaten.

Prita says:
GUD-JEE-YA (Gujiya)
DU-HE BULL-EE (Dahi Bhalle)

Savory foods, like dahi bhalle, are also eaten during the festival. Dahi bhalle are fried lentil balls that are eaten with yogurt and different sorts of chutney.

Love and Forgiveness

Holi is a festival about having fun, but it is also about forgiveness too. It is a time when people put their differences aside, forget old arguments and love one another.

At this time of year, everyone comes together and celebrates with their community and their loved ones. This is why Holi is also called the "festival of love."

Prita Says . . .

Brahman
BRA-MUN
Brahman is the true Hindu God.

Dahi Bhalle
DU-HE BULL-EE
Dahi Bhalle are fried lentil balls.

Dholak
DO-LUK
A dholak is a traditional hand drum.

Gujiya
GUD-JEE-YA
Gujiya are sweet dumplings filled with dry fruit and coconut.

Hiranyakashyap
HE-RAN-NAKAH-SHIP
Hiranyakashyap was a great king in India.

Holi Mubarak
HO-LEE MOO-BAH-RAK
Holi Mubarak means "Happy Holi" in Hindi.

Holika Dahan
HO-LEE-KA DA-HAN
Holika Dahan is the tradtion of lighting bonfires during Holi.

Prahlad
PRA-LAD
Prahlad was the great king Hiranyakashyap's son.

Vishnu
VISH-NOO
Vishnu is one of the
many Hindu gods.

Log on to www.av2books.com

AV² by Weigl brings you media enhanced books that support active learning. Go to www.av2books.com, and enter the special code found on page 2 of this book. You will gain access to enriched and enhanced content that supplements and complements this book. Content includes video, audio, weblinks, quizzes, a slide show, and activities.

AV² Online Navigation

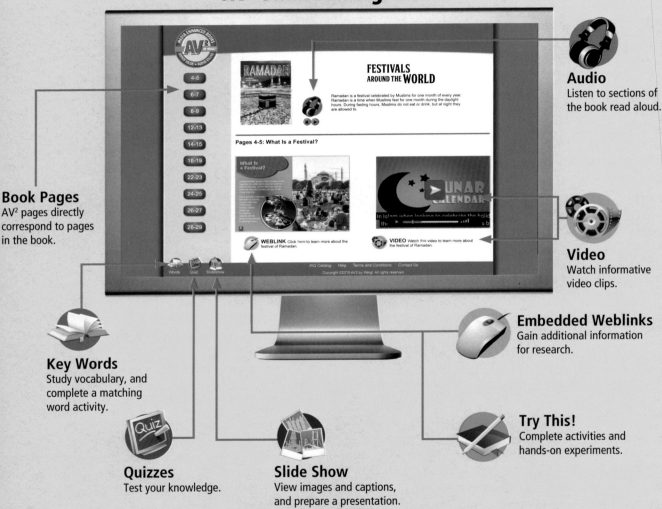

Audio
Listen to sections of the book read aloud.

Book Pages
AV² pages directly correspond to pages in the book.

Video
Watch informative video clips.

Key Words
Study vocabulary, and complete a matching word activity.

Embedded Weblinks
Gain additional information for research.

Quizzes
Test your knowledge.

Slide Show
View images and captions, and prepare a presentation.

Try This!
Complete activities and hands-on experiments.

AV² was built to bridge the gap between print and digital. We encourage you to tell us what you like and what you want to see in the future.

Sign up to be an AV² Ambassador at www.av2books.com/ambassador.